21st Century Junior Library

Get a Good Night's Sleep!

by Katie Marsico

CHERRY LAKE PUBLISHING * ANN ARBOR, MICHIGAN

CHERRY
LAKE
Publishing

Published in the United States of America by Cherry Lake Publishing
Ann Arbor, Michigan
www.cherrylakepublishing.com

Content Adviser: Kevin Allen, NASM - CPT, Metabolic Technician, Life Time Fitness, Novi, MI

Reading Adviser: Marla Conn, ReadAbility, Inc

Photo Credits: © kitty/Shutterstock Images, cover; © Golden Pixels LLC/Shutterstock Images, 4; © Donskaya Olga/Shutterstock Images, 6; © S-F/Shutterstock Images, 8; © Kamira/Shutterstock Images, 10; © Cristina Buldrini/Shutterstock Images, 12; © Hung Chung Chih/Shutterstock Images, 14; © Svetlana Foote/Shutterstock Images, 16; © Room27/Shutterstock Images, 18; © Pressmaster/ Shutterstock Images, 20

LIBRARY OF CONGRESS CATALOGING-IN-PUBLICATION DATA

Marsico, Katie, 1980-
  Get a good night's sleep!/By Katie Marsico.
      pages cm.—(Your healthy body)
  Includes index.
  Audience: 6-10
  Audience: K to grade 3
  ISBN 978-1-63188-988-2 (hardcover)—ISBN 978-1-63362-066-7 (pdf)—
ISBN 978-1-63362-027-8 (pbk.)—ISBN 978-1-63362-105-3 (ebook)
  1. Sleep—Juvenile literature. I. Title.
  RA786.M33 2015
  612.8'21—dc23   2014021531

*Cherry Lake Publishing would like to acknowledge the work of
The Partnership for 21st Century Skills.
Please visit www.p21.org for more information.*

Printed in the United States of America
Corporate Graphics

CONTENTS

Staying up late can be fun, but remember that you might feel tired tomorrow.

Why Bother with Bedtime?

Haley is running out of time! She has to go to bed at 8:00 p.m. But she knows her movie won't be finished by then. She begs her dad to let her stay up later. Besides, she isn't even tired. But Dad says she needs her rest.

Think! Think about when you go to bed. Think about when you wake up. How many hours of sleep do you get? Do you feel rested in the morning? Or do you feel like you need more sleep?

Sleep gives your mind and body a break.

People can't survive without sleep. During this rest period, they close their eyes. Soon they enter a state of **unconsciousness**. The body **refreshes** itself after a long period of being awake and active.

Sleep also helps a person fight off illness. The brain relies on sleep to work properly, too. The brain continues to produce **hormones** and organize information even during sleep.

Most kids between the ages of 5 and 12 need 10 to 11 hours of sleep a night.

Too little sleep makes it difficult to stay awake and remain focused.

Getting too little sleep affects a person's mood, **concentration**, and **coordination**. This causes simple activities to be harder to do than usual.

Make a Guess!

Are you able to guess how much sleep adults need? Did you answer 7 to 8 hours a night? You're right! Are you able to guess *why* adults require less sleep than kids?

Many people brush their teeth just
before they go to bed.

The Sleep Cycle

Dad promises Haley they'll finish the movie tomorrow. So she brushes her teeth and puts on her pajamas. Then her dad tucks her into bed.

Soon her eyelids start to feel heavy. Her brain is telling her body to slow down. This is the first stage in the sleep **cycle**. There are five stages, or steps, in total.

When you're sleeping, you aren't aware of anything going on around you.

The brain sends out signals that trigger muscles to relax. Body temperature and **blood pressure** start to drop slowly.

Sleep is deeper during stages two through four. People grow less aware of what is happening around them. Noises and movements are less likely to wake them up.

Stage five of the cycle involves rapid eye movement (REM) sleep. During that, people's eyes are closed but move back and forth quickly. Their heartbeat also speeds up, and their blood pressure rises.

Most people dream every night but don't remember their dreams the next day.

Their breathing becomes less regular. Stage five is also when people experience dreams: the thoughts, visions, and feelings that people have when asleep.

Different parts of a person's sleep cycle repeat between stage one and waking. Stages two through five return every 90 minutes. That's about six to seven times during 10 to 11 hours of sleep.

It's best to avoid sodas that contain caffeine before bedtime!

Ready to Wake Up Refreshed?

Haley is very tired, but also thirsty. She would like a cold soda.

But Dad explains that soda contains **caffeine**. So do chocolate, iced tea, and several others foods and drinks. Caffeine

Ask Questions! You read that caffeine can upset your sleep. What else affects your sleep? Is exercising before bed a good idea? How about eating sugary foods? Have an adult help you find answers online or at the library.

A clean bedroom makes it easier to relax.

often keeps people from sleeping. Water or milk are better choices in the evening.

Haley drinks some milk. What about finishing the movie, since she's still awake? But Dad says no.

He tells Haley her brain needs to begin winding down. The TV's lights and noises can interrupt the sleep cycle. Reading and

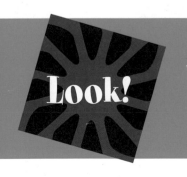

Look!

Look around your bedroom. What about it calms you and helps you fall asleep? Do you see anything that creates the opposite effect? What simple changes would improve how well you sleep?

Getting enough sleep will help you stay alert in school!

listening to soft music are calming bedtime activities. So is taking a warm bath.

Dad says people also sleep better if they stick to a **routine**. This means going to bed at the same time every night. Dad switches on Haley's night-light. He hugs her and wishes her sweet dreams.

The alarm clock rings at 7:00 the next morning. Haley got a good night's sleep. She feels refreshed and ready for school!

GLOSSARY

blood pressure (BLUHD PREH-shuhr) the force with which blood flows through a person's body

caffeine (kah-FEEN) a substance found in coffee, tea, and other food items that makes people feel more awake

concentration (kant-suhn-TRAY-shuhn) the ability to focus attention on a single object or activity

coordination (koh-or-duh-NAY-shuhn) the ability to move different body parts together gracefully and easily

cycle (SYE-kuhl) a series of events or actions that always recur in the same order

hormones (HOR-mohnz) natural substances produced by the body that affect how a person grows and develops

refreshes (ree-FRESH-uhz) causes someone to feel rested and energized

routine (roo-TEEN) a regular way of doing things in a certain order

unconsciousness (un-KAHNT-shuhs-nuhs) the state of being unawake and unaware of one's surroundings

FIND OUT MORE

BOOKS

Barraclough, Sue. *Sleep and Rest*. Mankato, MN: Sea-to-Sea Publications, 2012.

Kuskowski, Alex. *Cool Sleeping: Healthy and Fun Ways to Sleep Tight*. Minneapolis: ABDO Publishing Company, 2013.

Silverstein, Alvin, Virginia Silverstein, and Laura Silverstein Nunn. *Handy Healthy Guide to Better Sleep*. Berkeley Heights, NJ: Enslow Publishers, Inc., 2014.

WEB SITES

KidsHealth—What Sleep Is and Why All Kids Need It

kidshealth.org/kid/stay_healthy /body/not_tired.html#
Read more about the different stages of sleep, as well as how sleep affects your health.

National Sleep Foundation—Sleep for Kids

www.sleepforkids.org
Check out this site for online articles, games, and puzzles that focus on the importance of sleep.

INDEX

ABOUT THE AUTHOR

Katie Marsico is the author of more than 150 children's books. She lives in a suburb of Chicago, Illinois, with her husband and children.